for Meg love J.C.

Text and Illustrations © Jane Cabrera 2007
First published in Great Britain as *cat's cuddles* in 2007 by Gullane Children's Books,
an imprint of Pinwheel Limited, Winchester House, 259-269 Old Marylebone Road, London NW1 5XJ
First published in the United States of America by Holiday House, Inc. in 2007
Printed and Bound in china
www.holidayhouse.com
First Edition
1 3 5 7 9 10 8 6 4 2

Library of congress cataloging-in-Publication Data
Cabrera, Jane.
Kitty's cuddles / by Jane cabrera. — 1st ed.
p. cm.
First published in Great Britain in 2006 by Gullane children's Books.
Summary: Kitty tries out hugs from all different animals
but finds he likes the hug from his baby brother the best.
ISBN-13: 978-0-8234-2066-7 (hardcover)
[1. cats—Fiction. 2. Hugging—Fiction. 3. Animals—Fiction.] I. Title.
PZ7.C1135cdj 2007
[E]—dc22
2006049512

Kitty's Cuddles

Jane Cabrera

Holiday House / New York

I love cuddles!
But who is my favorite
friend to cuddle?

Is it Tiny Mouse

with his teeny-weeny cuddle?

Is it
Feathery
Peacock

with his bright,
tickly cuddle?

Is it Big **Bear**
with his cozy,
fluffy cuddle?

Is it Happy
Frog
with her squidgy,
quidgy cuddle?

Is it **Funny**
Monkey
with her tight,
treetop cuddle?

Is it Enormous Elephant with his big, strong cuddle?

Is it Soggy **Octopus** with his snug, squeezy cuddle?

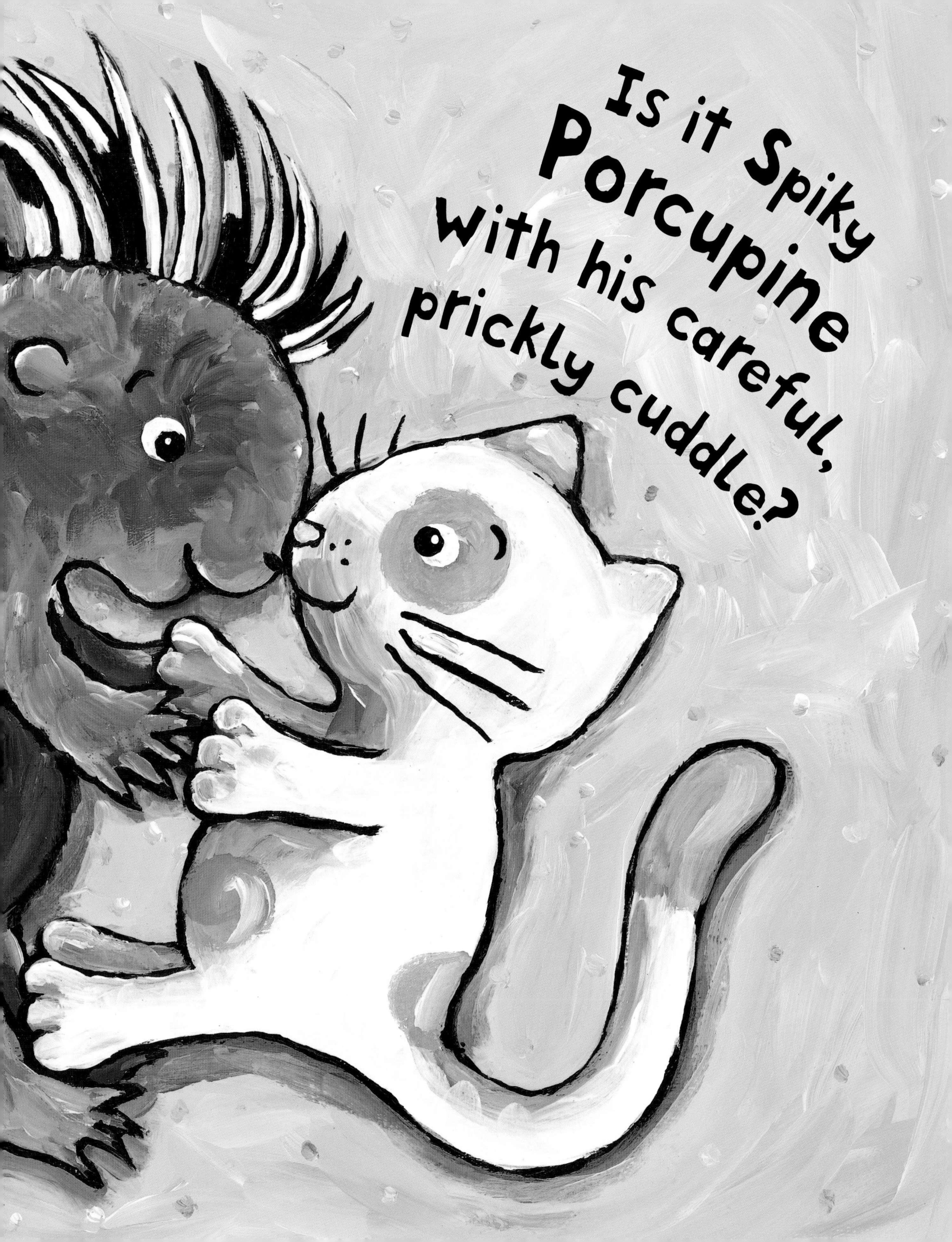

Is it Spiky Porcupine with his careful, prickly cuddle?

Is it Scaly
Armadillo
with her safe,
friendly cuddle?

Or is it
someone
very special

with the softest, warmest cuddle. . . .

Yes!
It's my new
baby brother!